137 150, 153
205

pp. 137, 150, 170, 205, 243
193

MONEY
AND
WEALTH

A BOOK OF QUOTATION$

EDITED BY JOSLYN PINE

DOVER PUBLICATIONS, INC. | MINEOLA, NEW YORK

At Dover Publications we're committed to producing books in an earth-friendly manner and to helping our customers make greener choices.

Manufacturing books in the United States ensures compliance with strict environmental laws and eliminates the need for international freight shipping, a major contributor to global air pollution. And printing on recycled paper helps minimize our consumption of trees, water and fossil fuels.

GREEN EDITION ®

The text of this book was printed on paper made with 10% post-consumer waste and the cover was printed on paper made with 10% post-consumer waste. At Dover, we use Environmental Defense's Paper Calculator to measure the benefits of these choices, including: the number of trees saved, gallons of water conserved, as well as air emissions and solid waste eliminated.

Courier Corporation, the manufacturer of this book, owns the Green Edition Trademark.

Please visit the product page for *Money and Wealth: A Book of Quotations* at **www.doverpublications.com** to see a detailed account of the environmental savings we've achieved over the life of this book.

Copyright

Copyright © 2013 by Dover Publications, Inc.
All rights reserved.

Bibliographical Note

Money and Wealth: A Book of Quotations is a new work, first published by Dover Publications, Inc., in 2013.

Library of Congress Cataloging-in-Publication Data

Money and wealth : a book of quotations / edited by Joslyn Pine.
    pages cm.
  ISBN-13: 978-0-486-48638-3
  ISBN-10: 0-486-48638-9
  1. Money—Quotations, maxims, etc. 2. Wealth—Quotations, maxims, etc. I. Pine, Joslyn.
PN6084.M56M656 2013
  332.4—dc23

                  2012033634

Manufactured in the United States by Courier Corporation
48638901
www.doverpublications.com

INTRODUCTION

Money is nothing more than an idea—a tool used as a measure to facilitate the exchange of goods and services. But *what* an idea and with what inordinate power it has been invested, to the point where it takes some effort to conceive of it as a mere abstraction—unless we think of the credit card, an American invention of the 1950s and "the most modern manifestation of money."[1]

At the dawn of human history, barter was probably the most widely used method of exchange, followed by the use of objects like cowrie shells and even chocolate—in the form of cacao beans—as currency. The earliest coins are believed to have been minted in the seventh century BC in the Asia Minor kingdom of Lydia, and from there the practice spread to other parts of the world. In fact, the expression "rich as Croesus" derived from the name of the Lydian king whose kingdom was especially prosperous, in large part due to these new and powerful tools of trade.[2] However, Spanish silver coins—pieces of eight—were the first

---

[1] Neil MacGregor, *A History of the World in 100 Objects: From the Handaxe to the Credit Card* (New York: Viking Penguin, 2011)

[2] Jack Weatherford, *The History of Money: From Sandstone to Cyberspace* (New York: Three Rivers Press, 1998).

global currency, initially minted in the 1570s and prevailing well into the nineteenth century on five continents.[3]

The origins of paper money were linked with the development of printing and papermaking in China, and may have been in use as early as the T'ang dynasty, AD 618–907, during a golden age when both the Chinese culture and economy flourished. However, it was the Americans who later advanced the widespread use of paper currency, most notably through the efforts of Ben Franklin, originally a printer by vocation, who not only printed some of the first money used in America, but also published a pamphlet on the subject of "the nature and necessity of a paper currency" in 1729.[4]

"There is no subject on which so much arrant nonsense has been written as on that of money."[5] And to avoid adding to that opus of "arrant nonsense," it was necessary to search far and wide, sometimes in obscure sources, to find quotations worthy of inclusion here. Part I of the book—Attributed Quotations: BC to the Present—is arranged chronologically by the birth year of the individual (and after that, alphabetically by last name in the instances of two

---

[3]MacGregor, *A History of the World in 100 Objects.*

[4]Weatherford, *The History of Money.*

[5]Friedrich August Wolf (1759–1824), German classical scholar and philologist.

or more individuals sharing the same birth year). Part II comprises random quotations from the Bible. And Part III consists of Proverbs—first organized alphabetically by the country of origin, followed by a Miscellaneous section arranged randomly.

One of the greatest challenges of compiling a book of quotes is finding worthy material that can stand on its own without an immediate context. That fact, to a significant extent, was a guiding principle in the selection of both the individuals and the quotations included. So the process by necessity had to be a purely subjective one. Excerpts from poetry and works of fiction are included, as well as song lyrics.

Since a wide variety of materials were used to compile this collection, spelling and punctuation have, for the most part, been modernized and standardized for the sake of clarity and consistency. Since four different sources might each contain a different version of the same quote, every effort has been made to present the version closest to the spirit and substance of the original.

Joslyn Pine
September 2011

MONEY
AND
WEALTH

A BOOK OF QUOTATION$

Money is life to us wretched mortals.

Little to little added, if oft done, in small time
makes a good possession.

Hesiod (c. 700 BC), Greek poet

Cursed be he above all others
Who's enslaved by love of money.
Money takes the place of brothers,
Money takes the place of parents,
Money brings us war and slaughter.

Anacreon (c. 582–485 BC), Greek poet

Do not work to make money for money's sake.

Buddha (c. 563–483 BC), Indian spiritual leader

Money can turn a lowly worm into a mighty dragon.

Money in the hands of a bachelor is as good as gone.

He who hasn't a penny sees bargains everywhere.

The gold does not belong to the miser,
but the miser to the gold.

The injury of prodigality leads to this, that he that
will not economize will have to agonize.

Confucius (551–479 BC), Chinese philosopher and teacher

For money, you would sell your soul.

You will see more ruined than saved by
money ill gotten.

Profit is sweet even if it comes from deception.

Sophocles (c. 496–406 BC), Greek playwright

Money is the wise man's religion.

Euripides (c. 484–406 BC), Greek playwright

Wealth is a lot of things
a man can do without.

Socrates (c. 470–399 BC),
Greek philosopher

Wealth is the parent of luxury and indolence,
and poverty of meanness and viciousness,
and both of discontent.

Plato (c. 427–347 BC), Greek philosopher

Money was intended to be used in exchange,
but not to increase at interest.

Aristotle (384–322 BC), Greek philosopher

No one gets rich quickly if he is honest.

Riches cover a multitude of woes.

Let him who weds wed character, not money.

Menander (c. 342–292 BC), Greek playwright

If thou wilt make a man happy, add not to his riches but take away from his desires.

Epicurus (341–270 BC), Greek philosopher

After spending some money in his sleep, Hermon the miser was so hopping mad he hanged himself.

Lucilius (c. 160–103 BC), Roman satirist

Above all is he admired who is not
influenced by money.

There is no sanctuary so holy that money
cannot profane it, no fortress so strong that
money cannot take it by storm.

Cicero (106–43 BC), Roman statesman, orator and writer

When reason rules, money is a blessing.

Everything is worth what its purchaser will pay for it.

Money does not sate Avarice, but stimulates it.

Fortune is like glass—the brighter the glitter,
the more easily broken.

Publilius Syrus (c. 100 BC), Latin poet and playwright

Make money: make it honestly if possible;
if not, make it by any means.

A heart well-prepared for adversity in bad
times hopes, and in good times fears
for a change in fortune.

Though you strut proud of your money,
yet fortune has not changed your birth.

Horace (65–8 BC), Roman poet and satirist

We feel public misfortunes just so far as
they affect our private circumstances, and
nothing of this nature appeals more directly
to us than the loss of money.

Livy (59 BC–AD 17), Roman historian

When every man worships gold,
all other reverence is done away.

Propertius (c. 50–after 16 BC), Roman poet

Money is now the prize.
Wealth in its train brings
honors, and brings friend-
ships; he who's poor is ever
cast aside.

Gold will buy the highest
honors; and gold will
purchase love.

Ovid (43 BC–AD 18), Roman poet

Not he who has little, but he who wishes more, is poor.

A good mind possesses a kingdom;
a great fortune is a great slavery.

Money does all things for reward. Some are pious and
honest as long as they thrive upon it, but if the devil
himself gives better wages, they soon change
their party.

Money is a greater torment in the possession, than it
is in the pursuit; the fear of losing it is a great trouble,
the loss of it a greater, and it is made a greater yet
by opinion.

Seneca (4 BC–AD 65), Roman philosopher and playwright

Fidelity bought with money is overcome by money.

The acquisition of riches has been to many not an
end to their miseries, but a change in them:
The fault is not in the riches, but the disposition.

What madness it is for a man to starve himself to
enrich his heir, and so turn a friend into an enemy!
For his joy at your death will be proportioned to
what you leave him.

Economy is too late when you are at the
bottom of your purse.

Seneca (4 BC–AD 65)

What power has law where only money rules?

Petronius Arbiter (?–c. AD 65), Roman satirist

It is a hard thing not to surrender morals for riches.

If you want him to mourn,
you had best leave him nothing.

Martial (c. AD 40–104), Roman poet

When the strong box contains no more,
both friends and flatterers shun the door.

Nothing is cheap which is superfluous, for what
one does not need, is dear at a penny.

Plutarch (c. AD 46–120), Greek biographer and philosopher

Lampis the shipowner, on being asked how he
acquired his great wealth, replied: "My great wealth
was acquired with no difficulty, but my small
wealth, my first gains, with much labor."

Epictetus (c. AD 55–135), Greek philosopher

The love of money grows with growing wealth.

Money lost is bewailed with unfeigned tears.

Juvenal (c. AD 55–130), Roman poet

Nothing that is God's is obtainable by money.

Tertullian (c. AD 160–230), Roman theologian

If you would get rid of a disagreeable person,
lend him money.

Francesco Accursius (1182–1260), Italian jurist and writer

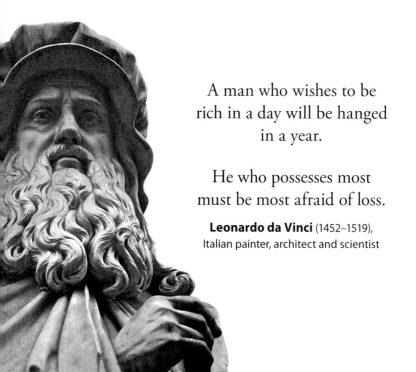

Love lasteth long as the money endureth.

William Caxton (c. 1422–1491), English writer, printer and diplomat

A man who wishes to be
rich in a day will be hanged
in a year.

He who possesses most
must be most afraid of loss.

Leonardo da Vinci (1452–1519),
Italian painter, architect and scientist

A little wanton money … burned out the
bottom of his purse.

Sir Thomas More (1478–1535),
English writer, statesman and theologian

The god of this world is riches, pleasure,
and pride, wherewith it abuses all the creatures
and gifts of God.

Martin Luther (1483–1546), German theologian and teacher

He left a paper sealed up, wherein were found three articles as his last will, "I owe much, I have nothing, I give the rest to the poor."

François Rabelais (c. 1494–1553), French writer and humanist

Bad money drives out good. [Gresham's law]

Sir Thomas Gresham (1519–1579), English philosopher and banker

With money you would not know yourself; without money no one would know you.

The money paid, the work delayed.

Miguel de Cervantes (1547–1616), Spanish novelist, poet and playwright

Money is like muck, not good except it be spread.

No man's fortune can be an end worthy of his being.

If money be not thy servant, it will be thy master. The covetous man cannot so properly be said to possess wealth, as that it may be said to possess him.

The fortune which nobody sees makes a person happy and unenvied.

Of great wealth there is no real use, except in its distribution, the rest is just conceit.

Be not penny-wise; riches have wings, and sometimes they fly away of themselves, sometimes they must be set flying to bring in more.

Francis Bacon (1561–1626), English philosopher and statesman

Excess of wealth is cause of covetousness.

Christopher Marlowe (1564–1593), English poet and playwright

This yellow slave
Will knit and break religions; bless the accurs'd;
Make the hoar leprosy ador'd; place thieves,
And give them title, knee, and approbation,
With senators on the bench.

If money go before, all ways do lie open.

If thou art rich, thou art poor;
For like an ass, whose back with ingots bows
Thou bearest thy heavy riches but a journey,
And death unloads thee.

I had rather than forty shillings, I had my book of
songs and sonnets here.

If thou wilt lend this money, lend it not
As to thy friends …
But lend it rather to thine enemy,
Who, if he break, thou mayst with better face
Exact the penalty.

O, what a world of vile ill-favour'd faults looks
handsome in three hundred pounds a year!

Well, whiles I am a beggar, I will rail,
And say, there is no sin, but to be rich;
And being rich, my virtue then shall be
To say, there is no vice, but beggary.

He that dies, pays all debts.

William Shakespeare (1564–1616), English poet and playwright

Money thou need'st:
'Twill keep thee honest; want made thee a knave.

Ben Jonson (1572–1637), English playwright

If thou wouldst keep money, save money;
if thou wouldst reap money, sow money.

Be the business never so painful,
you may have it done for money.

Help me to money and I'll help myself to friends.

God makes, and apparel shapes: but it's money
that finishes the man.

Thomas Fuller (1608–1661), English theologian, writer and historian

Let none admire that riches grow in hell;
that soil may best deserve the precious bane.

John Milton (1608–1674), English poet and essayist

War requires three things—money, money, money.

Montecucculi (c. 1608–1680), Italian military leader

'Tis virtue, wit, and worth, and all
That men divine and sacred call:
For what is worth in anything,
But so much money as 'twill bring?

'Tis true we've money, th' only power that
all mankind falls down before.

Wealth is nothing in itself; it is not useful but
when it departs from us.

Money and time are the heaviest burdens of life,
and the unhappiest of all mortals are those who have
more of either than they know how to use.

Money has a power above the stars and fate,
to manage love.

Samuel Butler (1612–1680), English poet and satirist

Money does all things; for it gives and takes away, it makes honest men and knaves, fools and philosophers; and so forward, mutatis mutandis, to the end of the chapter.

Sir Roger l'Estrange (1616–1704), English journalist and essayist

Money was made not to command our will, but
all our lawful pleasures to fulfill; shame and woe
to us, if we our wealth obey—the horse doth
with the horseman run away.

Abraham Cowley (1618–1667), English poet and essayist

If we from wealth to poverty descend, want
gives to know the flatterer from the friend.

Go miser go, for money sell your soul. Trade
wares for wares and trudge from pole to pole,
so others may say when you are dead and gone.
See what a vast estate he left his son.

Fortune befriends the bold.

John Dryden (1631–1700), English poet and playwright

Money makes up in a measure all other wants in men.

William Wycherley (c.1640–1715), English playwright

If making money is a slow process,
losing it is quickly done.

Ihara Saikaku (1642–1693), Japanese poet and novelist

The spendthrift robs his heirs, the miser robs himself.

Jean de la Bruyère (1645–1696), French essayist

Riches are a burden … There is a burden of care in getting them, fear in keeping them, temptation in using them, guilt in abusing them, sorrow in losing them, and a burden of account at last to be given up concerning them.

Matthew Henry (1662–1714), English theologian and biblical scholar

Money is the lifeblood of the nation.

A wise man should have money in his head,
but not in his heart.

Jonathan Swift (1667–1745), Anglo-Irish novelist and satirist

Gold is a wonderful clearer of the understanding;
it dissipates every doubt and scruple in an instant,
accommodates itself to the meanest capacities,
silences the loud and clamorous, and brings over
the most obstinate and inflexible.

Joseph Addison (1672–1719), English poet, playwright and essayist

Let all the learned say all they can,
'Tis ready money makes the man.

William Somerville (1675-1742), English poet

Money is the sinews of love, as of war.

George Farquhar (1678–1707), Irish playwright

Can wealth give happiness? look round and see
What gay distress! what splendid misery!
Whatever fortune lavishly can pour,
The mind annihilates, and calls for more.

Edward Young (1683–1765), English poet and playwright

Why lose we life in anxious cares,
To lay in hoards for future years?
Can those (when tortur'd by disease)
Cheer our sick heart, or purchase ease?
Can those prolong one gasp of breath,
Or calm the troubled hour of death?

John Gay (1688–1732), English poet and playwright

But Satan now is wiser than of yore, and tempts
by making rich, not making poor.

Trade it may help, society extend,
But lures the pirate, and corrupts the friend;
It raises armies in a nation's aid,
But bribes a senate, and the land's betray'd.

Alexander Pope (1688–1744), English poet and satirist

When it is a question of money, everybody
is of the same religion.

It is easier to write on money than to obtain it,
and those who gain it, jest much at those who only
know how to write about it.

Voltaire (1694–1778), French novelist, poet and playwright

A light purse is a heavy curse.

Wealth is not his that has it, but his that enjoys it.

If you would know the value of money, go and try
to borrow some; for he that goes a-borrowing
goes a-sorrowing.

He that is of the opinion money will do
everything may well be suspected of doing
everything for money.

If you would be wealthy, think of saving
as well as getting.

Beware of little expenses; a small leak will sink
a great ship.

Benjamin Franklin (1706–1790),
American writer, diplomat and scientist

Money never made a man happy yet, nor will it. There is nothing in its nature to produce happiness. The more a man has, the more he wants. Instead of its filling a vacuum, it makes one. If it satisfies one want, it doubles and trebles that want another way.

If you'd lose a troublesome visitor, lend him money.

There are three faithful friends: an old wife, an old dog, and ready money.

A little house well filled, a little field well tilled, and a little wife well willed, are great riches.

If your riches are yours, why don't you take them with you to the other world?

Remember that time is money.

A man who multiplies riches, multiplies cares.

If you know how to spend less than you get, you have the philosopher's stone.

The use of money is all the advantage there is in having money.

Benjamin Franklin (1706–1790)

Money is the fruit of evil as often as the root of it.

Money, money, the most charming of all things; money, which will say more in one moment than the most elegant lover can in years. Perhaps you will say a man is not young; I answer he is rich. He is not genteel, handsome, witty, brave, good-humored, but he is rich, rich, rich, rich, rich—that one word contradicts everything you can say against him.

If you make money your god, it will plague you like the devil.

Henry Fielding (1707–1754), English novelist

HENRY FIELDING, Ætat XLVIII.

H. Fielding

It is better to live rich than to die rich.

The lust of gold succeeds the rags of conquest:
The lust of gold unfeeling and remorseless!
The last corruption of degenerate man.

No man but a blockhead ever wrote except for money.

Money can neither open up new avenues to pleasure,
nor block up the passages of anguish.

To purchase Heaven has gold the power?
Can gold remove the mortal hour?
In life can love be bought with gold?
Are friendship's pleasures to be sold?

Wealth is nothing in itself, it is not useful but
when it departs from us.

Samuel Johnson (1709–1784), English writer and lexicographer

Money is not, properly speaking, one of the subjects of commerce, but only the instrument which men have agreed upon to facilitate the exchange of one commodity for another.

David Hume (1711–1776), Scottish philosopher and historian

Money is the seed of money and the first guinea is sometimes more difficult to acquire than the second million.

Jean-Jacques Rousseau (1712–1778), French philosopher

A miser grows rich by seeming poor.
An extravagant man grows poor by seeming rich.

William Shenstone (1714–1763), English poet

Money is oftentimes the only patent of nobility,
beside lofty pretensions.

Johann Georg Zimmermann (1728–1795),
Swiss philosopher, writer and physician

If we command our wealth, we shall be rich
and free; if our wealth commands us,
we are poor indeed.

Edmund Burke (1729–1797),
Anglo-Irish philosopher and statesman

Ill fares the land, to hast'ning ills a prey,
where wealth accumulates, and men decay.

Oliver Goldsmith (1730–1774),
Anglo-Irish novelist, poet and playwright

It is not a custom with me to keep money to look at.

To contract new debts is not the way to pay old ones.

George Washington (1732–1799), first U.S. president

The rich are seldom remarkable for modesty, ingenuity, or humanity. Their wealth has rather a tendency to make them penurious and selfish.

All the perplexities, confusions, and distress in America arise, not from defects in their constitution or confederation, not from want of honor or virtue, so much as from the downright ignorance of the nature of coin, credit, and circulation.

John Adams (1735–1826), second U.S. president

To despise money is to dethrone a king.

Preoccupation with money is the great test of small natures, but only a small test of great ones.

Society is composed of two great classes, those who have more dinners than appetite, and those who have more appetite than dinners.

Sébastien-Roch Nicolas Chamfort (1740–1794),
French playwright and essayist

I have not observed men's honesty to increase with their riches.

Money, not morality, is the principle of commercial nations.

Never spend your money before you have it.

It is neither wealth nor splendor, but tranquility and occupation, which give happiness.

Thomas Jefferson (1743–1826), third U.S. president

I sincerely believe that banking establishments are more dangerous than standing armies, and that the principle of spending money to be paid by posterity, under the name of funding, is but swindling futurity on a large scale.

Never buy a thing you do not want, because it is cheap; it will be dear to you.

Take care of your cents: Dollars will take care of themselves.

Thomas Jefferson (1743–1826)

Many people take no care of their money
till they come nearly to the end of it, and others
do just the same with their time.

Johann von Goethe (1749–1832),
German playwright, poet and polymath

Want of money and the distress of a thief can
never be alleged as the cause of his thieving, for
many honest people endure greater hardships
with fortitude. We must therefore seek the cause
elsewhere than in want of money, for that is the
miser's passion, not the thief's.

Christianity is art and not money.
Money is its curse.

William Blake (1757–1827), English poet and painter

The circulation of confidence is better than
the circulation of money.

James Monroe (1758–1831), fifth U.S. president

No man needs money so much as a man
who despises it.

Johann Paul Friedrich Richter (1763–1825),
German novelist (pseud. Jean Paul)

There is some magic in wealth, which can thus make persons pay their court to it, when it does not even benefit themselves. How strange it is, that a fool or knave, with riches, should be treated with more respect by the world, than a good man, or a wise man in poverty!

Ann Radcliffe (1764–1823), English novelist

The pride of dying rich raises the loudest laugh in hell.

John Foster (1770–1843), English clergyman and essayist

In the bad old days, there were three easy ways of losing money—racing being the quickest, women the pleasantest and farming the most certain.

William Pitt Amherst (1773–1857),
English diplomat and Governor-General of India

Business, you know, may bring money,
but friendship hardly ever does.

Nothing amuses me more than the easy manner
with which everybody settles the abundance of
those who have a great deal less than themselves.

A large income is the best recipe for
happiness I ever heard of.

When money is once parted with,
it can never return.

Jane Austen (1775–1817), English novelist

O money, money, how blindly thou hast been worshipped, and how stupidly abused!

Charles Lamb (1775–1834), English essayist

Money is a bottomless sea, in which honor, conscience, and truth may be drowned.

Ivan Kozlov (1779–1840), Russian poet

Riches may enable us to confer favors, but to confer them with propriety and grace requires a something that riches cannot give.

It is only when the rich are sick that they fully feel the impotence of wealth.

There is this difference between those two temporal blessings, health and money: Money is the most envied, but the least enjoyed; health is the most enjoyed, but the least envied: and this superiority of the latter is still more obvious when we reflect that the poorest man would not part with health for money, but that the richest would gladly part with all their money for health.

Many speak the truth when they say that they despise riches, but they mean the riches possessed by other men.

Charles Caleb Colton (c. 1780–1832), English writer and clergyman

Hate, religion, ambition, all have their hypocrisies,
but money applies the thumbscrew to them all.

George Croly (1780–1860), Irish poet, writer and clergyman

The almighty dollar, that great object of universal
devotion throughout our land.

Washington Irving (1783–1859),
American short story writer, essayist and historian

Ready money is Aladdin's lamp.

Mammon wins his way where
seraphs might despair.

Those who declaim loudest against money-
getting are often the most avaricious.

Lord (George Gordon) Byron (1788–1824), English poet

Money is human happiness in the abstract:
he, then, who is no longer capable of enjoying
human happiness in the concrete devotes his
heart entirely to money.

Wealth is like sea-water; the more we drink,
the thirstier we become.

Arthur Schopenhauer (1788–1860), German philosopher

Money is often lost for want of money.

Zadock Pratt (1790–1871), American politician and entrepreneur

Commerce has set the mark of selfishness, the signet of its all-enslaving power, upon a shining ore, and called it gold.

There is no real wealth but the labor of man.

Percy Bysshe Shelley (1792–1822), English poet

The deepest depth of vulgarism is that of setting up
money as the ark of the covenant.

Money, in truth, can do much, but it cannot do all.
We must know the province of it, and confine it there,
and even spurn it back when it wishes to get farther.

Thomas Carlyle (1795–1881), Scottish essayist and historian

Money is a necessity; so is dirt.

Thomas Chandler Haliburton (1796–1865),
Canadian writer, jurist and politician

Money is the god of our time.

Heinrich Heine (1797–1856), German poet and essayist

The art of living easily as to money is to pitch your scale of living one degree below your means.

Sir Henry Taylor (1800–1886), English playwright

Money is a terrible blab; she will betray the secrets of her owner, whatever he do to gag her; his virtues will creep out in her whisper, his vices she will cry aloud at the top of her tongue.

Character is money; and according as the man earns or spends the money, money in turn becomes character. As money is the most evident power in the world's uses, so the use that he makes of money is often all that the world knows about a man.

Sir Edward Bulwer-Lytton (1803–1873),
English poet, playwright and novelist

Money, which represents the prose of life, and which is hardly spoken of in parlors without an apology, is, in its effects and laws, as beautiful as roses.

The value of a dollar is social, as it is created by society.

He is only rich who owns the day.

Money often costs too much.

Can anybody remember when the times were not hard and money not scarce?

Money is of no value; it cannot spend itself.
All depends on the skill of the spender.

Ralph Waldo Emerson (1803–1882), American poet and writer

As men advance in life, all passions resolve themselves into money. Love, ambition, even poetry, end in this.

Benjamin Disraeli (1804–1881), English writer and politician

It is my opinion that a man's soul may be buried and perish under a dung-heap, or in a furrow of the field, just as well as under a pile of money.

Nathaniel Hawthorne (1804–1864),
American novelist and short story writer

I know of no country [i.e., America], indeed,
where the love of money has taken stronger hold
on the affections of men, and where a profounder
contempt is expressed for the theory of the
permanent equality of property.

Alexis de Tocqueville (1805–1859), French historian and statesman

That some should be rich shows that others may become rich and hence is just encouragement to industry and enterprise.

Abraham Lincoln (1809–1865), sixteenth U.S. president

The Romans worshipped their standard; and the Roman standard happened to be an eagle. Our standard is only one-tenth of an eagle—a dollar— but we make all even by adoring it with tenfold devotion.

Edgar Allan Poe (1809–1849), American poet and writer

Money is a terrible master but an excellent servant.

Money-getters are the benefactors of our race.

P. T. Barnum (1810–1891), American showman and entrepreneur

The darkest hour of any man's life is when he sits down
to plan how to get money without earning it.

Horace Greeley (1811–1872), American newspaper editor and politician

Annual income twenty pounds, annual expenditure nineteen six, result happiness. Annual income twenty pounds, annual expenditure twenty pound ought and six, result misery.

Credit is a system whereby a person who can't pay gets another person who can't pay to guarantee that he can pay.

Dollars! All their cares, hopes, joys, affections, virtues, and associations seemed to be melted down into dollars. … Men were weighed by their dollars, measures were gauged by their dollars; life was auctioned, appraised, put up, and knocked down for its dollars. The next respectable thing to dollars was any venture having their attainment for its end.

Charles Dickens (1812–1870), English writer

Money will buy you a pretty good dog,
but it won't buy the wag of his tail.

Money is like promises—easier made
than kept.

It ain't often that a man's reputation
outlasts his money.

Henry Wheeler Shaw (1815–1885),
American writer-humorist

A man is rich in proportion to the things
he can afford to let alone.

Money is not required to buy one necessity
of the soul.

Almost any man knows how to earn money,
but not one in a million knows how to spend it.

If you give money, spend yourself with it.

Henry David Thoreau (1817–1862),
American essayist and naturalist

Capital is money, capital is commodities. …
By virtue of it being value, it has acquired the occult
ability to add value to itself. It brings forth living
offspring, or, at the least, lays golden eggs.

Money is the external, universal means and power
(not derived from man as man nor from human
society as society) to change representation into
reality and reality into mere representation.

While the miser is merely a capitalist gone mad,
the capitalist is a rational miser.

Karl Marx (1818–1883), German philosopher and revolutionary

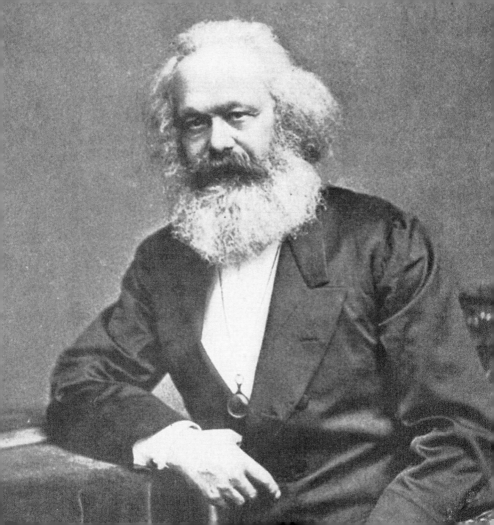

The urbane activity with which a man receives money
is really marvelous, considering that we so earnestly
believe money to be the root of all earthly ills.

Herman Melville (1819–1891), American novelist

Money is only thus far a standard of value;
that which it can measure is perishable;
that which it cannot is immortal.

Christian Nestell Bovee (1820–1904), American jurist and writer

A man who hoards up riches and enjoys them not is
like an ass that carries gold and eats thistles.

Sir Richard Francis Burton (1821–1890), English scholar, poet and explorer

Business? It's quite simple. It's other people's money.

Alexandre Dumas, fils (1824–1895), French novelist and playwright

Men who are deaf to the claims of mercy, and oblivious to the demands of justice, can feel when money is slipping from their pockets.

Frances Ellen Watkins Harper (1825–1911), American poet and novelist

There is a vast difference in one's respect for the man who has made himself, and the man who has only made his money.

Dinah Mulock Craik (1826–1887), English novelist and poet

Money may be the husk of many things but not the kernel. It brings you food, but not appetite; medicine, but not health; acquaintance, but not friends; servants, but not loyalty; days of joy, but not peace or happiness.

Henrik Ibsen (1828–1906), Norwegian playwright

Money is a new form of slavery, and distinguishable from the old simply by the fact that it is impersonal—that there is no human relation between master and slave.

Leo Tolstoy (1828–1910), Russian novelist and essayist

Money is honey, my little sonny,
and a rich man's joke is always funny.

Thomas Edward Brown (1830–1897), English poet and theologian

I am an advocate of paper money, but that paper
money must represent what it professes on its face.
I do not wish to hold in my hands
the printed lies of government.

He who controls the money supply of a nation
controls the nation.

James A. Garfield (1831–1881), twentieth U.S. president

Money is the root of all evil, and yet it is such a useful root that we cannot get on without it any more than we can without potatoes.

Louisa May Alcott (1832–1888), American novelist

Economy is half the battle of life. It is not so hard to earn money as to spend it well.

Charles Haddon Spurgeon (1834–1892), English preacher and writer

It has been said that the love of money is the root of all evil. The want of money is so quite as truly.

When you have told anyone you have left him a legacy, the only decent thing to do is to die at once.

Money is the last enemy that shall never be subdued. While there is flesh there is money—or the want of money; but money is always on the brain so long as there is a brain in reasonable order.

Brigands demand your money or your life; women require both.

Samuel Butler (1835–1902), English novelist and essayist

Money can only be the useful drudge of things immeasurably higher than itself. Exalted beyond this, as it sometimes is, it remains Caliban still and still plays the beast.

Public sentiment will come to be that the man who dies rich dies disgraced.

Andrew Carnegie (1835–1919), American industrialist

Virtue has never been as respectable as money.

His money is twice tainted: 'taint yours
and 'taint mine.

Honesty is the best policy—when there is money in it.

Make money and the whole world will conspire
to call you a gentleman.

A dollar picked up in the road is more satisfaction to
us than the ninety-nine which we had to work for,
and the money won at Faro or in the stock market
snuggles into our hearts in the same way.

Some men worship rank, some worship heroes,
some worship power, some worship God, & over these
ideals they dispute & cannot unite—but they all
worship money.

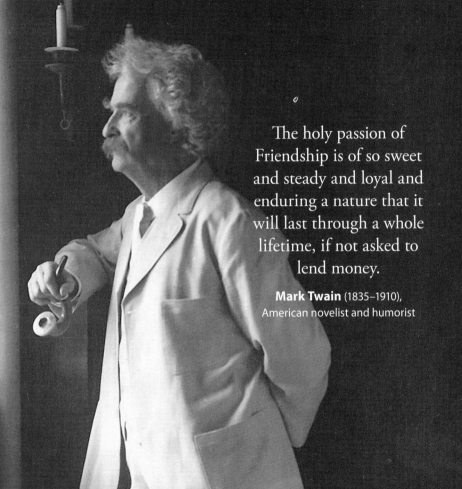

The holy passion of Friendship is of so sweet and steady and loyal and enduring a nature that it will last through a whole lifetime, if not asked to lend money.

Mark Twain (1835–1910), American novelist and humorist

God gave me my money. I believe the power
to make money is a gift from God—to be
developed and used to the best of our ability
for the good of mankind.

John D. Rockefeller (1839–1937),
American entrepreneur and philanthropist

It isn't enough for you to love money—it's also necessary that money should love you.

A banker is a man who lends another man the money of a third man.

Baron de Rothschild (1840–1915),
English banker and politican

A man is usually more careful of his money than of his principles.

Put not your trust in money, but put your money in trust.

Oliver Wendell Holmes (1841–1935),
American jurist, historian and philosopher

Money, n. A blessing that is of no advantage to us excepting when we part with it. An evidence of culture and a passport to polite society.

Philanthropist, n. A rich (and usually bald) old gentleman who has trained himself to grin while his conscience is picking his pocket.

Ambrose Bierce (1842– c. 1914),
American short story writer and journalist

Money's a horrid thing to follow,
but a charming thing to meet.

Henry James (1843–1916), American novelist

In every well-governed state, wealth is
a sacred thing; in democracies it is the
only sacred thing.

Anatole France (1844–1924), French novelist and essayist

Money alone is only a means; it presupposes a man
to use it. The rich man can go where he pleases, but
perhaps please himself nowhere. … The purse may be
full and the heart empty. He may have gained
the world and lost himself.

The price we have to pay for money
is sometimes liberty.

Robert Louis Stevenson (1850–1894), Scottish novelist, poet and essayist

It's a grand thing to be able to take your money in your hand and to think no more of it when it slips away from you than you would a trout that would slip back into a stream.

Lady Augusta Gregory (1852–1932), Irish playwright and folklorist

There is only one thing for a man to do who is married to a woman who enjoys spending money, and that is to enjoy earning it.

No man's credit is ever as good as his money.

When a man says money can do anything, that settles it. He hasn't any.

Edgar Watson Howe (1853–1937), American novelist and journalist

When I was young I thought that money was the most important thing in life; now that I am old I know that it is.

It is better to have a permanent income than to be fascinating.

There is only one class in the community that thinks more about money than the rich, and that is the poor. The poor can think of nothing else.

Oscar Wilde (1854–1900), Anglo-Irish playwright, writer and poet

Riches are the savings of many in the hands of one.

Eugene V. Debs (1855–1926), American labor leader

Gentlemen prefer bonds.

Andrew Mellon (1855–1937), American financier

This will never be a civilized country until
we spend more money for books than we
do for chewing gum.

Money never made a fool of anybody;
it only shows them up.

Elbert Hubbard (1856–1915),
American writer, artist and publisher

Money is indeed the most important thing in the world; and all sound and successful personal and national morality should have this fact for its basis.

Better see rightly on a pound a week than squint on a million.

The lack of money is the root of all evil.

George Bernard Shaw (1856–1950), Irish playwright and critic

"Time is money"—says the vulgarest saw known to any age or people. Turn it round about, and you get a precious truth—money is time.

Money is time. With money I buy for cheerful use the hours which otherwise would not in any sense be mine; nay, which would make me their miserable bondsman.

George Gissing (1857–1903), English novelist

To rail at money, to wax indignant against it, is silly. Money is nothing; its power is purely symbolical. Money is the sign of liberty. To curse money is to curse liberty—to curse life, which is nothing, if it be not free.

Remy de Gourmont (1858–1915), French poet, novelist and essayist

When money stands still, it is no longer money.

Georg Simmel (1858–1918), German philosopher and sociologist

Money is round. It rolls away.

Sholem Aleichem (1859–1916), Yiddish writer and playwright

No man can earn a million dollars honestly.

William Jennings Bryan (1860–1925), American statesman and orator

Nothing links man to man like the frequent passage from hand to hand of cash.

Walter Sickert (1860–1942), English artist

Money, what is money? It is only loaned to a man; he comes into the world with nothing and leaves with nothing.

William ("Billy") Crapo Durant (1861–1947), American industrialist

The greed of gain has no time or limit to its capaciousness. Its one object is to produce and consume. It has pity neither for beautiful nature nor for living human beings. It is ruthlessly ready without a moment's hesitation to crush beauty and life out of them, molding them into money.

Rabindranath Tagore (1861–1941),
Bengali poet, writer, painter and composer

You can't appreciate home until you've left it, money till it's spent, your wife till she's joined a woman's club, nor Old Glory till you see it hanging on a broomstick on the shanty of a consul in a foreign town.

O. Henry (1862–1910), American short story writer

The only way not to think about money
is to have a great deal of it.

Edith Wharton (1862–1937), American writer

Money is just what we use to keep tally.

Money does not change men, it only unmasks them.
If a man is naturally selfish or arrogant or greedy,
the money brings that out, that's all.

The highest use of capital is not to make more money,
but to make money do more for the betterment of life.

If money is your hope for independence you will
never have it. The only real security that a man can
have in this world is a reserve of knowledge,
experience and ability.

Money is like an arm or leg—use it or lose it.

A business that makes nothing but money is
a poor kind of business.

Henry Ford (1863–1947), American industrialist and entrepreneur

In suggesting gifts: Money is appropriate,
and one size fits all.

William Randolph Hearst (1863–1951), American newspaper tycoon

We have become ninety-nine percent money mad.
The method of living at home modestly and within
our income, laying a little by systematically for the
proverbial rainy day which is due to come,
can almost be listed among the lost arts.

George Washington Carver (1864–1943),
American scientist, inventor and educator

The notion of making money by popular work, and then retiring to do good work on the proceeds, is the most familiar of all the devil's traps for artists.

Those who set out to serve both God and Mammon soon discover that there isn't a God.

The wretchedness of being rich is that you live with rich people. To suppose, as we all suppose, that we could be rich and not behave as the rich behave, is like supposing that we could drink all day and stay sober.

Most people sell their souls, and live with a good conscience on the proceeds.

Logan Pearsall Smith (1865–1946), American man of letters

Much ingenuity with a little money is vastly
more profitable and amusing than much
money without ingenuity.

Arnold Bennett (1867–1931), English novelist and playwright

On John D. Rockefeller: He's kind of a society for
the prevention of cruelty to money. If he finds a
man misusing his money he takes it away
from him and adopts it.

Finley Peter Dunne (1867–1936), American humorist and journalist

It's good to have money and the things that money can buy, but it's good, too, to check up once in a while and make sure that you haven't lost the things that money can't buy.

George H. Lorimer (1867–1937), American writer and editor

The insolence of authority is endeavoring to substitute money for ideas.

Frank Lloyd Wright (1867–1959), American architect

When a fellow says, "It ain't the money, but the principle of the thing," it's the money.

It ain't no disgrace to be poor, but it might as well be.

The safest way to double your money is to fold it over and put it in your pocket.

Frank McKinney ("Kin") Hubbard
(1868–1930), American journalist and humorist

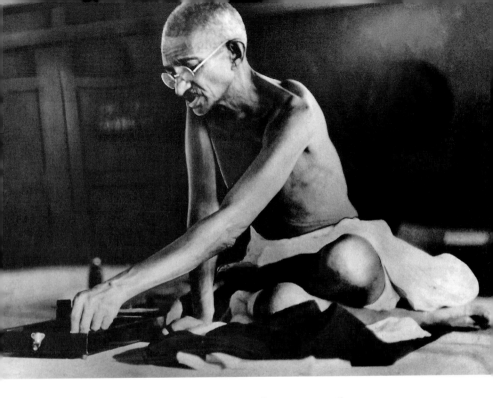

Money as such is not evil;
it is its wrong use that is evil.

Mahatma Gandhi (1869–1948), Indian political and spiritual leader

Advertising may be described as the science of
arresting the human intelligence long enough
to get money from it.

Stephen Leacock (1869–1944),
Canadian humorist, writer and economist

I'm tired of Love: I'm still more tired of Rhyme.
But Money gives me pleasure all the time.

Hilaire Belloc (1870–1953), English writer, poet and historian

I had made up my mind that since I was not going to be a Negro, I would avail myself of every possible opportunity to make a white man's success; and that, if it can be summed up in any one word, means "money."

James Weldon Johnson (1871–1938),
American poet, writer and social activist

Nothing is easier than spending the public money. It does not appear to belong to anybody. The temptation is overwhelming to bestow it on somebody.

Calvin Coolidge (1872–1933), thirtieth U.S. president

Money is a great dignifier.

Paul Laurence Dunbar (1872–1906),
American poet, writer and lyricist

If you would know what the Lord God thinks
of money, you have only to look at those to
whom he gives it.

Maurice Baring (1874–1945), English journalist and novelist

To be clever enough to get all that money,
one must be stupid enough to want it.

Gilbert Keith Chesterton (1874–1936), English writer, journalist and artist

Saving is a very fine thing. Especially when
your parents have done it for you.

Sir Winston Churchill (1874–1965),
English prime minister, writer and historian

There are few sorrows, however poignant,
in which a good income is of no avail.

Never ask of money spent
Where the spender thinks it went.
Nobody was ever meant
To remember or invent
What he did with every cent.

Robert Frost (1874–1963), American poet

One of the greatest disservices you can do a man is to lend him money that he can't pay back.

Jesse H. Jones (1874–1956), American politician and entrepreneur

Money is like a sixth sense, and you can't make use of the other five without it.

Money is the string with which a sardonic destiny directs the motion of its puppets.

W. Somerset Maugham (1874–1965), English novelist

Whoever said money can't buy happiness
didn't know where to shop.

The thing that differentiates man
from animals is money.

Money is always there but the pockets change;
it is not in the same pockets after a change,
and that is all there is to say about money.

Gertrude Stein (1874–1946), American expatriate writer

A fool and her money are soon courted.

Helen Rowland (1875–1950), American journalist

Money is the only substance which can keep a cold
world from nicknaming a citizen "Hey, you!"

Wilson Mizner (1876–1933), American playwright and entrepreneur

There is nothing so habit-forming as money.

Don Marquis (1878–1937), American writer, poet and humorist

Money is power, freedom, a cushion,
the root of all evil, the sum of blessings.

Carl Sandburg (1878–1967), American poet

The state is or can be master of money,
but in a free society it is master of very little else.

William Henry Beveridge (1879–1963), English economist

Too many of us look upon Americans as dollar
chasers. This is a cruel libel, even if it is reiterated
thoughtlessly by the Americans themselves.

Albert Einstein (1879–1955), German scientist and writer

Lord, the money we do spend on Government and it's not one bit better than the government we got for one-third the money twenty years ago.

Let advertisers spend the same amount of money improving their product that they do on advertising and they wouldn't have to advertise it.

Will Rogers (1879–1935), American humorist and actor

A rich man is nothing but a poor man with money.

W. C. Fields (1880–1946), American actor and comedian

The chief value of money lies in the fact that one lives in a world in which it is overestimated.

No one in this world, so far as I know—and I have searched the records for years, and employed agents to help me—has ever lost money by underestimating the intelligence of the great masses of the plain people.

H. L. Mencken (1880–1956), American journalist and man of letters

Money, like number and law, is a category of thought.

Oswald Spengler (1880–1936), German writer, historian and philosopher

The modern banking system manufactures
money out of nothing. The process is perhaps
the most astounding piece of sleight-of-hand
that was ever invented.

Josiah Charles Stamp (1880–1941),
English economist, banker and writer

Why is there so much month left
at the end of the money?

John Barrymore (1882–1942), American actor

To have money is to be virtuous, honest,
beautiful and witty. And to be without it is
to be ugly, boring, stupid and useless.

Jean Giraudoux (1882–1944), French novelist and playwright

Money may kindle, but it cannot by itself,
and for very long, burn.

Igor Stravinsky (1882–1971), Russian composer

A woman must have money and a room of her
own if she is to write fiction.

Money dignifies what is frivolous if unpaid for.

Virginia Woolf (1882–1941), English novelist and essayist

There are people who have money
and people who are rich.

Coco Chanel (1883–1971), French fashion designer

Money is like love; it kills slowly and painfully
the one who withholds it, and it enlivens the
other who turns it upon his fellow man.

The virtue of some of the rich is that
they teach us to despise wealth.

Kahlil Gibran (1883–1931),
Lebanese-American writer, poet and philosopher

If I owe you a pound, I have a problem; but if I owe you a million, the problem is yours.

Most men love money and security more, and creation and construction less, as they get older.

The moral problem of our age is concerned with the love of money.

John Maynard Keynes (1883–1946), English economist

Nothing that costs only a dollar is worth having.

Elizabeth Arden (1884–1966), American entrepreneur

When money talks, few are deaf.

Earl Derr Biggers (1884–1933), American writer and playwright

The only difference between the rich and other people is that the rich have more money.

Mary Colum (1884–1957), Irish writer and literary critic

Always try to rub up against money, for if you rub up against money long enough, some of it may rub off on you.

Damon Runyan (1884–1946), American short story writer and journalist

Three things ruin a man. Power, money, and women.
I never wanted power. I never had any money, and the
only woman in my life is up at the house right now.

Harry S Truman (1884–1972), thirty-third U.S. president

I've been poor and I've been rich. Rich is better.

From birth to eighteen, a girl needs good parents. From eighteen to thirty-five, she needs good looks. From thirty-five to fifty-five, she needs a good personality. From fifty-five on, she needs good cash.

Sophie Tucker (1884–1966), American vaudeville singer

Money is our madness, our vast collective madness.

D. H. Lawrence (1885–1930), English novelist, poet and essayist

Dollars do better if they are accompanied by sense.

Earl Riney (1885–1955), American clergyman

Nothing is more admirable than the fortitude with which millionaires tolerate the disadvantages of their wealth.

Rex Stout (1886–1975), American mystery writer

The petty economies of the rich are just as amazing as the silly extravagances of the poor.

Wealth flows from energy and ideas.

A budget tells us what we can't afford, but it doesn't keep us from buying it.

William A. Feather (1889–1981), American writer and publisher

Some people think they are worth a lot of money
just because they have it.

Fannie Hurst (1889–1968), American writer

Well, fancy giving money to the Government!
Might as well have put it down the drain.
Fancy giving money to the Government!
Nobody will see the stuff again.
Well, they've no idea what money's for—
Ten to one they'll start another war.

A. P. Herbert (1890–1971), English novelist, playwright and humorist

Money frees you from doing things you dislike.
Since I dislike doing nearly everything,
money is handy.

Groucho Marx (1890–1977), American actor-comedian and TV host

I can't imagine having so little faith in the Lord,
and so much faith in money, that you would end
your life over a little thing like losing your fortune.

Money is at the root of every mess you can think of,
including slavery.

Bessie Delany (1891–1995), American writer and civil rights activist

I was part of that strange race of people, aptly described as spending their lives doing things they detest to make money they don't want to buy things they don't need to impress people they dislike.

Emile Henry Gauvreau (1891–1956), American writer, reporter and editor

I have no money, no resources, no hopes.
I am the happiest man alive.

Henry Miller (1891–1980), American writer and painter

If you can actually count your money
you are not really a rich man.

Money is like manure. You have to spread it around
or it smells.

J. Paul Getty (1892–1976), American entrepreneur and art philanthropist

When it comes to finances, remember that there
are no withholding taxes on the wages of sin.

Mae West (1893–1980), actress and comedienne

Those who have some means think that the most important thing in the world is love. The poor know that it is money.

Gerald Brenan (1894–1987), English writer and historian

I'm living so far beyond my income that we may almost be said to be living apart.

E. E. Cummings (1894–1962), American poet

If there's no money in poetry, neither is there poetry in money.

Robert Graves (1895–1985), English poet and novelist

One of the penalties of wealth is that the older you grow, the more people there are in the world who would rather have you dead than alive.

C. H. B. Kitchin (1895–1967), English novelist

On the ten million dollars he earned and spent during his career: Part of the loot went for gambling, part for horses, and part for women. The rest I spent foolishly.

George Raft (1895–1980), American actor and dancer

A billion here, a billion there, and pretty soon you're talking about real money.

Everett M. Dirksen (1896–1969), American politician

Let me tell you about the very rich. They are different from you and me. They possess and enjoy early, and it does something to them, makes them soft where we are hard, and cynical where we are trusting.

Her voice is full of money.

F. Scott Fitzgerald (1896–1940), American novelist

Where there is money there is fighting.

Marian Anderson (1897–1993), American opera singer

Money is something you got to make in case
you don't die.

Max Asnas (1897–1968), American entrepreneur

Where money talks, there are few interruptions.

Herbert V. Prochnow (1897–1998), American banker and writer

Life is short and so is money.

Bertolt Brecht (1898–1956), German playwright and poet

If a man runs after money, he's money-mad; if he keeps it, he's a capitalist; if he spends it, he's a playboy; if he doesn't get it, he's a ne'er-do-well; if he doesn't try to get it, he lacks ambition. If he gets it without working for it, he's a parasite; and if he accumulates it after a lifetime of hard work, people call him a fool who never got anything out of life.

Vic Oliver (1898–1964), actor and radio personality

Empty pockets never held anyone back.
Only empty heads and empty hearts can do that.

Norman Vincent Peale (1898–1993),
American religious leader and writer

Never invest your money in anything that eats
or needs repairing.

Billy Rose (1899–1966), American songwriter and producer

Economy is a way of spending money without getting
any pleasure out of it.

Armand Salacrou (1899–1989), French playwright

There is a strange and mighty race of people called the
Americans who are rapidly becoming the coldest in the
world because of this cruel, man-eating idol, lucre.

Edward Dahlberg (1900–1977), American novelist and essayist

There was a time when a fool and his money were soon parted, but now it happens to everybody.

Adlai E. Stevenson (1900–1965), American statesman

You have reached the pinnacle of success as soon as you become uninterested in money, compliments, or publicity.

Thomas Wolfe (1900–1938), American novelist

Why rob banks? That's where the money is.

Willie Sutton (1901–1980), American bank robber

People who work sitting down get paid more than people who work standing up.

The only incurable troubles of the rich are the troubles that money can't cure.

Some people's money is merited
And other people's is inherited.

Ogden Nash (1902–1971), American poet-humorist

A bank is a place that will lend you money
if you can prove that you don't need it.

Bob Hope (1903–2003), American comedian and actor

A woman's best protection is a little money of her own.

Claire Boothe Luce (1903–1987),
American playwright, journalist and politician

Money isn't everything—but it's a long way ahead of what comes next.

Edmund Stockdale (1903–1989),
English baronet and Lord Mayor of London

Liking money like I like it, is nothing less than mysticism. Money is a glory.

Salvador Dalí (1904–1989), Spanish artist

The trouble with being poor is that it takes up all your time.

Willem de Kooning (1904–1997), Dutch-American artist

Money is what you'd get on beautifully without if only other people weren't so crazy about it.

Margaret Case Harriman (c. 1904–1966), writer and social critic

Money is not an aphrodisiac; the desire it may kindle in the female eye is more for the cash than the carrier.

Marya Mannes (1904–1990), American writer and critic

Money and women … they're the two strongest things in the world. The things you do for a woman you wouldn't do for anything else. Same with money.

Satchel Paige (c. 1905–1982), American Major League Baseball player

We women ought to put first things first. Why should we mind if men have their faces on the money, as long as we get our hands on it?

Ivy Baker Priest (1905–1975), American politican

Money is only a tool. It will take you wherever you wish, but it will not replace you as the driver.

Money is your means of survival. The verdict you pronounce upon the source of your livelihood is the verdict you pronounce upon your life. If the source is corrupt, you have damned your own existence.

So you think that money is the root of all evil. Have you ever asked what is the root of all money?

Ayn Rand (1905–1982), American writer and philosopher

We invented money and we use it, yet we cannot either understand its laws or control its actions.

Lionel Trilling (1905–1975),
American writer, literary critic and educator

Power can be thought of as the never-ending, self-feeding motor of all political action that corresponds to the legendary unending accumulation of money that begets money.

Hannah Arendt (1906–1975),
American writer and political philosopher

That money talks
I'll not deny,
I heard it once:
It said, "Goodbye."

Richard Armour (1906–1989), American poet and writer

I've got all the money I'll ever need if I die
by four o'clock.

You can't buy love, but you can pay heavily for it.

Americans are getting stronger. Twenty years ago,
it took two people to carry ten dollars' worth of
groceries. Today, a five-year-old can do it.

Henny Youngman (1906–1998), American comedian and violinist

If you're given a choice between money and
sex appeal, take the money. As you get older,
the money will become your sex appeal.

Katharine Hepburn (1907–2003), American actress

The farmer's way of saving money:
to be owed by someone he trusted.

Hugh MacLennan (1907–1990), Canadian writer and essayist

Ben Franklin may have discovered electricity, but it was the man who invented the meter who made the money.

Isn't it a shame that future generations can't be here to see all the wonderful things we're doing with their money?

No horse can go as fast as the money you put on it.

Money in the bank is like toothpaste in the tube. Easy to take out, hard to put back.

Earl Wilson (1907–1987), American writer and newspaper columnist

I'd marry again if I found a man who had fifteen million dollars, would sign over half to me, and guarantee that he'd be dead within a year.

Bette Davis (1908–1989), American actress

Money is a singular thing. It ranks with love as man's greatest source of joy. And with death as his greatest source of anxiety. Over all history it has oppressed nearly all people in one of two ways: either it has been abundant and very unreliable, or reliable and very scarce.

If the history of commercial banking belongs to the Italians and of central banking to the British, that of paper money issued by a government belongs indubitably to the Americans.

Money differs from an automobile or mistress in being equally important to those who have it and those who do not.

Wealth is not without its advantages and the case to the contrary, although it has often been made, has never proved widely persuasive.

John Kenneth Galbraith (1908–2006), American economist and scholar

No woman marries for money; they are all clever enough, before marrying a millionaire, to fall in love with him first.

Cesare Pavese (1908–1950), Italian writer and poet

Money can't buy happiness, but neither can poverty.

Leo Rosten (1908–1997), American writer, humorist and educator

Keep company with the very rich and you'll
end up picking up the check.

Stanley Walker (1908–1993), English cricketer

Any man who has $10,000 left when he dies
is a failure.

Errol Flynn (1909–1959), American actor

Bankruptcy is a legal proceeding in which you
put your money in your pants pocket and give
your coat to your creditors.

Joey Adams (1911–1999), American comedian

Money is just the poor man's credit card.

Marshall McLuhan (1911–1980), Canadian writer and philosopher

Money can't buy happiness, but it will get
you a better class of memories.

Ronald Reagan (1911–2004), actor and fortieth U.S. president

Money is good for bribing yourself through the inconveniences of life.

Gottfried Reinhardt (1911–1994), German film director

You can be young without money,
but you can't be old without it.

Tennessee Williams (1911–1983), American playwright and poet

One is always excited by descriptions of money changing hands. It's much more fundamental than sex.

Nigel Dennis (1912–1989), English writer, playwright and journalist

Inflation is taxation without legislation.

Milton Friedman (1912–2006), American economist

The money complex is the demonic, and the demonic is God's ape; the money complex is therefore the heir to and substitute for the religious complex, an attempt to find God in things.

Norman O. Brown (1913–2002), American philosopher

The society of money and exploitation has never been charged, so far as I know, with assuring the triumph of freedom and justice.

It's a kind of spiritual snobbery that makes people think they can be happy without money.

Albert Camus (1913–1960), French novelist, journalist and philosopher

Money—in its absence we are coarse;
in its presence we are vulgar.

Too much money is as demoralizing as too little,
and there's no such thing as exactly enough.

Mignon McLaughlin (1913–1983), American writer and journalist

Money never remains just coins and pieces of paper.
Money can be translated into the beauty of living, a
support in misfortune, an education, or future security.
It can also be translated into a source of bitterness.

Sylvia Porter (1913–1991), American economist and journalist

We live by the Golden Rule. Those who have the gold make the rules.

Buzzie Bavasi (1914–2008),
American Major League Baseball executive

Everything costs a lot of money when you haven't got any.

I don't like money actually, but it quiets my nerves.

Joe Louis (1914–1981),
American World Heavyweight boxing champion

If God has allowed me to earn so much money,
it is because He knows I give it all away.

Édith Piaf (1915–1963), French singer and actress

Money won't buy happiness, but it will pay
the salaries of a large research staff to study
the problem.

Bill Vaughan (1915–1977), American writer and journalist

Gentility is what is left over from rich
ancestors after the money is gone.

John Ciardi (1916–1986), American poet and essayist

One man's wage rise is another man's price increase.

Harold Wilson (1916–1995), English prime minister

Men make counterfeit money; in many more cases,
money makes counterfeit men.

Sydney J. Harris (1917–1986), American writer and newpaper columnist

If a person gets his attitude toward money straight,
it will help straighten out almost every other area
in his life.

Billy Graham (born 1918), American evangelist and writer

Money can't buy friends, but it can get you
a better class of enemy.

All I ask is the chance to prove that money
can't make me happy.

Spike Milligan (1918–2002), English comedian, musician and writer

Poor people have more fun than rich people, they say.
But I notice it's the rich people who keep saying it.

Jack Paar (1918–2004), American TV personality

Finance is the art of passing money from hand
to hand until it finally disappears.

Robert W. Sarnoff (1918–1997), American media executive

Money is the most egalitarian force in society.
It confers power on whoever holds it.

Roger Starr (1918–2001), American writer and city planner

Money is one of the shatteringly simplifying ideas
of all time.

Paul J. Bohannan (1920–2007), American anthropologist

A poor person who is unhappy is in a better position
than a rich person who is unhappy. Because the poor
person has hope. He thinks money would help.

Jean Kerr (1922–2003), American writer and playwright

Money is the mother's milk of politics.

Jesse M. Unruh (1922–1987), American politician

Money you haven't earned is not good for you.

Robert Maxwell (1923–1991), English publisher

Money, it turned out, was exactly like sex. You thought of nothing else if you didn't have it and thought of other things if you did.

James Baldwin (1924–1987), American expatriate novelist and playwright

A nickel ain't worth a dime anymore.

Yogi Berra (born 1925), American Major League Baseball player and manager

We ought to change the legend on our money from "In God We Trust" to "In Money We Trust." Because, as a nation, we've got far more faith in money these days than we do in God.

Arthur Hoppe (1925–2000), American newspaper journalist

No one would remember the Good Samaritan if he'd only had good intentions—he had money too.

It is not the creation of wealth that is wrong, but the love of money for its own sake.

Margaret Thatcher (born 1925), English prime minister

The greatest pleasure when I started making money was not buying cars or yachts but finding myself able to have as many freshly typed drafts as possible.

Gore Vidal (1925–2012), American writer and essayist

Writing is turning one's worst moments into money.

When you don't have any money, the problem is food.
When you have money, it's sex.
When you have both, it's health.

J. P. Donleavy (born 1926), Irish-American writer

I don't want to make money. I just want to be wonderful.

Marilyn Monroe (1926–1962), American actress

Money won't make you happy, but everybody wants to find out for themselves.

Zig Ziglar (1926–2012), American writer and motivational speaker

If you marry for money, you will surely earn it.

Ezra Bowen (c. 1927–1996), American writer and editor

No, not rich. I am a poor man with money, which is not the same thing.

Gabriel Garcia Marquez (born 1928), Colombian-Mexican writer

You can have money piled up to the ceiling but the size of your funeral is still going to depend on the weather.

Chuck Tanner (1928–2011),
American Major League Baseball player and manager

Making money is art and working is art and good business is the best art.

Andy Warhol (1928–1987), American artist

The trouble with paper money is that it rewards the minority that can manipulate money and makes fools of the generation that has worked and saved.

George Goodman (born 1930), American economist and writer (pseud. Adam Smith)

Rule No. 1: Never lose money.
Rule No. 2: Never forget rule No. 1.

I want to give my kids just enough so that they would feel that they could do anything, but not so much that they would feel like doing nothing.

Of the billionaires I have known, money just brings out the basic traits in them. If they were jerks before they had money, they are simply jerks with a billion dollars.

Warren Buffet (born 1930),
American entrepreneur, financier and philanthropist

It's not whether you are right or wrong that's important, but how much money you make when you're right and how much you lose when you're wrong.

George Soros (born 1930), American financier

He made his money the really old-fashioned way. He inherited it.

AJ Carothers (1931–2007), American playwright and screenwriter

Money makes the world go around.

Fred Ebb (1932–2004), American songwriter

The entire essence of America is the hope to first make money—then make money with money—then make lots of money with lots of money.

Paul Erdman (1932–2007), American business and financial writer

Wealth takes away the sharp edges of our moral sensitivities and allows a comfortable confusion about sin and virtue.

Henri J. M. Nouwen (1932–1996), Dutch priest and writer

Politics doesn't control the world, money does.

Andrew Young (born 1932), American politician, diplomat and writer

You must get money to chase you,
but never let it catch up.

Denis Waitley (born 1933), American writer and motivational speaker

Having money is rather like being a blond.
It is more fun but not vital.

Mary Quant (born 1934), English fashion designer

It is more rewarding to watch money change
the world than watch it accumulate.

Gloria Steinem (born 1934), American writer, journalist and feminist

Money is better than poverty,
if only for financial reasons.

Woody Allen (born 1935), American filmmaker and writer-humorist

Through money or power you cannot solve all
problems. The problem in the human heart must
be solved first.

Dalai Lama (born 1935), Tibetan religious leader and Nobel laureate

Money is like fire, an element as little troubled by moralizing as earth, air and water. Men can employ it as a tool or they can dance around it as if it were the incarnation of a god.

Seeing is believing, and if an American success is to count for anything in the world it must be clothed in the raiment of property. As often as not it isn't the money itself that means anything; it is the use of money as the currency of the soul.

Lewis H. Lapham (born 1935), American writer and editor

I have enough money to last me the rest of my life, unless I buy something.

Jackie Mason (born 1936), American comedian

Money will determine whether the accused goes to prison or walks out of the courtroom a free man.

Johnnie Cochran (1937–2005), American jurist

Money is a mechanism for control.

David Korten (born 1937), American economist, writer and educator

She had money and she had connections. Connections were more important than money. But money and connections both—that was unbeatable.

Raymond Carver (1938–1988), American short story writer and poet

The only people who claim that money is not important are people who have enough money so that they are relieved of the ugly burden of thinking about it.

Joyce Carol Oates (born 1938), American novelist and educator

Few women care to be laughed at and men not at all,
except for large sums of money.

Alan Ayckbourn (born 1939), English playwright

The shortest period of time lies between the minute
you put some money away for a rainy day and
the unexpected arrival of rain.

Jane Bryant Quinn (born 1939), American financial journalist

No matter how hard you hug your money,
it never hugs back.

H. Jackson Brown, Jr. (born 1940), American writer

Successful people make money. It's not that people who make money become successful, but that successful people attract money. They bring success to what they do.

Wayne Dyer (born 1940), American writer and lecturer

When you ain't got no money,
you gotta get an attitude.

Life doesn't change when you start making money;
you have the same problems you always had.

Richard Pryor (1940–2005), American comedian, actor and writer

Money doesn't talk, it swears.

What's money? A man is a success if he gets up in the morning and gets to bed at night, and in between he does what he wants to.

Bob Dylan (born 1941), American poet, singer and songwriter

I don't care too much for money,
money can't buy me love.

Paul McCartney (born 1942) and **John Lennon** (1940–1980),
English singer-songwriters

The power of money is a distinctly male power.
Money speaks, but it speaks with a male voice.

Andrea Dworkin (1946–2005), American writer and feminist

Money lets you live better.
It doesn't make you play better.

Reggie Jackson (born 1946), American Major League Baseball player

Money was never a big motivation for me,
except as a way to keep score. The real
excitement is playing the game.

Donald Trump (born 1946),
American financial tycoon and TV personality

Money, of course, is never just money. It's always something else, and it's always something more, and it always has the last word.

Paul Auster (born 1947), American novelist, poet and essayist

Money doesn't make you happy. I now have fifty
million dollars but I was just as happy
when I had forty-eight million.

Arnold Schwarzenegger (born 1947), American actor and politician

Money doesn't mind if we say it's evil, it goes from strength to strength. It's a fiction, an addiction, and a tacit conspiracy.

Weapons are like money; no one knows the meaning of *enough*.

Martin Amis (born 1949), English writer

Inflation is when you pay fifteen dollars for the ten-dollar haircut you used to get for five dollars when you had hair.

Sam Ewing (born 1949), American Major League Baseball player

Making money is fun, but it's pointless if
you don't use the power it brings.

John Bentley (born 1951), English rock musician

Cocaine is God's way of telling you
you have too much money.

Robin Williams (born 1951), American actor and comedian

Libraries will get you through times of
no money better than money will get you
through times of no libraries.

Anne Herbert (born 1952), American writer and editor

If money is your motivation, forget it.

Oprah Winfrey (born 1954),
American TV personality, actress and entrepreneur

Without money, you have no control.
Without control, you have no power.

Spike Lee (born 1957), American film director and writer

[Rap] is the last step of the civil rights movement.
You know—wrap your hands around some money.

Russell Simmons (born 1957), American arts entrepreneur

All sins are forgiven once you start making
a lot of money.

RuPaul (born 1960), American entertainer and drag queen

If I weren't earning three million dollars a year to dunk a basketball, most people on the street would run in the other direction if they saw me coming.

Charles Barkley (born 1963), American NBA basketball player

I'm tired of hearing about money, money, money, money, money. I just want to play the game, drink Pepsi, wear Reebok.

I don't believe that I personally have been changed by the money. … The bad thing is people assume you've been changed because now you have money.

Shaquille O'Neal (born 1972), American NBA basketball player and rapper

A feast is made for laughter, and wine maketh merry: but money answereth all things.

It is easier for a camel to go through the eye of a needle, than for a rich man to enter into the kingdom of God.

He that trusteth in his riches shall fall.

A good name is rather to be chosen than great riches.

For the love of money is the root of all evil: which while some coveted after, they have erred from the faith, and pierced themselves through with many sorrows.

Thy money perish with thee, because thou has thought that the gift of God may be purchased with money.

A rich man's wealth is his strong city;
the poverty of the poor is their ruin.

There is no riches above a sound body.

If riches increase, set not your heart
upon them.

It is better to give alms than to lay up gold.

A little that a righteous man hath is better
than the riches of many wicked.

Watching for riches consumeth the flesh,
and the care thereof driveth away sleep.

Riches certainly make themselves wings;
they fly away as an eagle toward heaven.

As the partridge sitteth on eggs and
hatcheth them not; so he that getteth
riches, and not by right, shall leave them
in the midst of his days, and at his end
shall be a fool.

How much better is it to get wisdom
than gold!

Giveth me neither poverty nor riches.

The idols of the heathen are silver and gold,
the work of men's hands.

Riches and strength lift up the heart.

The poor man is honored for his skill,
and the rich man is honored for his riches.

Wealth maketh many friends; but the poor is separated from his neighbor.

Neither their silver nor their gold shall be able to deliver them in the day of their Lord's wrath.

Ye cannot serve God and mammon.

PART III
PROVERBS

The big bee flies high, the little bee make the honey; the black folks makes the cotton, and the white folks get the money.

Nothing can suffice a person except that which they have not.

African-American proverbs

Only when the last tree has died and the last river been poisoned and the last fish caught will we realize we cannot eat money.

American (Cree) Indian proverb

With money one may command devils;
without it one cannot even summon a man.

By filling one's head instead of one's pocket,
one cannot be robbed.

If you are poor, though you dwell in the busy
marketplace, no one will inquire about you; if
you are rich, though you dwell in the heart of
the mountains, you will have distant relatives.

One who does not receive just wages
will seek to pay himself.

Our needs are few, but our wants
increase with our possessions.

He that is without money might as well be
buried in a rice tub with his mouth sewed up.

When a man obtains a large sum,
without having earned it, if it does not
make him very happy, it will certainly
make him very unhappy.

One who marries for money must
eventually earn it.

Chinese proverbs

To know you have enough is to be rich.

Those who make money make little
exertion; those who make much exertion
make no money.

When the man of a naturally good propensity
has much wealth, it injures his advancement
in wisdom; when the worthless man has
much wealth, it increases his faults.

Poverty without complaint is hard,
just as wealth with arrogance is easy.

Illness can empty any purse.

To buy a quarrel, lend money to a friend.

With money you can buy a house, but not a home.
With money you can buy a clock, but not time.
With money you can buy a bed, but not sleep.
With money you can buy a book, but not knowledge.
With money you can buy a doctor, but not good health.
With money you can buy position, but not respect.
With money you can buy blood, but not life.
With money you can buy sex, but not love.

Chinese proverbs

Money is more eloquent than a dozen
members of parliament.

One handful of money is stronger than
two handfuls of truth.

As water runs toward the shore,
so does money toward the rich man's hand.

Danish proverbs

He who lends money to a friend,
is sure to lose both.

To know the value of money,
one must be obliged to borrow it.

A man without money is like
a wolf without teeth.

A man is rich who owes nothing.

He that spends more than he is worth
spins a rope for his own neck.

Ready money works great cures.

Do not lend your money to a great man.

French proverbs

Gold rules the world.

The thirst for money brings all the sins
into the world.

Money lent to a friend must be
recovered from an enemy.

Money taken, freedom forsaken.

Where there's money there's the devil,
but where there's none a greater evil.

German proverbs

Money swore an oath that nobody who
did not love it should ever have it.

Irish proverb

Public money is like holy water;
everyone helps himself to it.

Italian proverb

Getting money is like digging with a needle.
Spending it is like water soaking into sand.

Money grows on the tree of persistence.

When life is ruined for the sake of money's
preciousness, the ruined life cares naught
for the money.

You will lack nothing if you think privation
is always with you.

When you have money, think of the time
when you had none.

Money matters make strangers.

Japanese proverbs

With money in your pocket, you are wise,
and you are handsome, and you sing well too.

A man who will pay has the say.

Because of money, the world became ugly.

The longest road in the world is the one that
leads to the pocket.

Sooner ask a man for his life than for
his money.

Money never cometh out of season.

Why is man born with hands clinched, but
has his hands wide open in death? On entering
the world man desires to grasp everything, but
when leaving it he takes nothing away.

Jewish proverbs

Much coin, much care.

Money, like a queen, gives rank and beauty.

Money is first to be sought, virtue afterwards.

Latin proverbs

Fortune favors the brave.

Mexican proverb

When I had money,
everyone called me brother.

Polish proverb

Laws go where dollars please.

Money is not gained by losing time.

Good manners and plenty of money will
make my son a gentleman.

Money is the measure of all things.

Portuguese proverbs

The rich would have to eat money,
but luckily the poor provide food.

No man is hanged who has money
in his pocket.

Russian proverbs

Money is flat and meant to be piled up.

A penny saved is a penny gained.

A moneyless man goes fast through
the market.

He who marries for love without money,
hath merry nights and sorry days.

Get what you can and keep what you have.
That's the way to get rich.

Scottish proverbs

A man that is rich will not be called a fool.

Spanish proverb

To beg of the miser is to dig a trench
in the sea.

If a man's money be white no matter if
his face is black.

My money is little, my heart without strife.

Turkish proverbs

MISCELLANEOUS PROVERBS

(ANONYMOUS/UNATTRIBUTED)

Money is an article which may be used as a universal passport to everywhere except Heaven, and as a universal provider of everything but happiness.

There are some things that money cannot buy.

Intaxication: Euphoria at getting a refund from the IRS, which lasts until you realize it was your money to start with.

Put your money where your mouth is.

Just pretending to be rich
keeps some people poor.

You can't take it with you when you go.

Trust not your money to one whose eyes
are bent on the ground.

Money will make the pot boil though
the devil pour water on the fire.

The abundance of money ruins youth.

Who heeds not a penny shall never have any.

After a man gets rich, his next ambition
is to get richer.

Money doesn't talk these days.
It goes without saying.

If your outgo exceeds your income,
then your upkeep will be your downfall.

He that hoardeth up money
taketh pains for other men.

When honor grew mercenary,
money grew honorable.

Profits are an opinion, cash is a fact.

Beauty is potent but money is omnipotent.

Money can't buy health, happiness,
or what it did last year.

Once upon a time only Washington's face
was on our money. Now Washington's
hands are on it too.

My neighbor accused his wife of spending
money like a drunken sailor. Is that any worse
than spending like a sober Congressman?

By the time a man has money to burn,
the fire has gone out.

Borrow money from a pessimist—
they don't expect it back.

Anyone can be great with money. With money,
greatness is not a talent but an obligation.
The trick is to be great without money.

Two can live as cheaply as one,
but only half so long.

The fellow that has no money is poor.
The fellow that has nothing but money
is poorer still.

Don't lend people money,
it gives them amnesia.

The buck stopped before it got to me.

In the old days a man who saved money
was a miser; nowadays he's a wonder.

A fool may make money, but it needs
a wise man to spend it.

The miser and the pig are of no use
to the family till dead.

If the risk-reward ratio is right,
you can make big money buying trouble.

Money can't buy happiness;
it can, however, rent it.

Money doesn't grow on trees;
you've got to beat the bushes for it.

A money-grabber is anyone who grabs
more money than you can.

Gold goes in any gate except heaven's.

Money is the best bait to fish for man with.

Nowadays a miser is one who lives
within his income.

If you're going to lend money, make sure
somebody else is around. If you're going to
give money, make sure nobody else is around.

There's a way of transferring funds that
is even faster than electronic banking.
It's called marriage.

When money speaks the truth is silent.

Money talks, but it doesn't always talk sense.

Penny wise is often pound foolish.

Money burns a hole in the pocket.